J 952 Lee
Lee, Adrienne
Samurai

$25.99
ocn830683502
05/13/2014

Legendary Warriors

by Adrienne Lee

Reading Consultant:
Barbara J. Fox
Professor Emerita
North Carolina State University

CAPSTONE PRESS
a capstone imprint

Blazers Books are published by Capstone Press,
1710 Roe Crest Drive, North Mankato, Minnesota 56003
www.capstonepub.com

Library of Congress Cataloging-in-Publication Data
Lee, Adrienne, 1981–
      Samurai / by Adrienne Lee.
      pages cm.—(Blazers books. Legendary warriors)
      Includes index.
      Summary: "Describes the lives of Japan's Samurai warriors, including their daily life, weapons,
and fighting techniques"—Provided by publisher.
      ISBN 978-1-4765-3113-7 (library binding)
      ISBN 978-1-4765-3371-1 (ebook pdf)
      1. Samurai—Japan—Juvenile literature. I. Title.
DS827.S3L45 2014
952—dc23   2013010447

Editorial Credits
Megan Peterson and Mandy Robbins, editors; Kyle Grenz, designer; Wanda Winch, media researcher;
Jennifer Walker, production specialist

Photo Credits
Alamy Images: Iain Masterton, 29; The Bridgeman Art Library: ©Look and Learn/Private Collection,
5, 17, ©Look and Learn/Private Collection/Dan Escott, 25 (bottom), ©Look and Learn/Private
Collection/Pat (Patrick) Nicolle, 12, 18, Fitzwilliam Museum, University of Cambridge, UK/Ogata
Gekko, 15; Library of Congress: Prints and Photographs Division, 26, 27; Newscom: akg-images/
©Sotheby's, 11, World History Archive, 6; Shutterstock: Antonio Agrignani, 14, 21 (b), Canicula, 28,
Jandi Attila, cover (Samurai), Marc Dietrich, 19, Maxim Tupikov, 8–9, Micha Klootwijk, cover, 1 (sai),
Papik, 21 (top), szefei, cover (background), Vudhikrai, cover, 1 (bottom sword); Wikimedia: Rama,
25 (top); Wikipedia: User LordAmeth, Collection of The Town of Sekigahara Archive of History and
Cultural Anthropology, Japan, 22–23

Printed in the United States of America in Stevens Point, Wisconsin.
032013   007227WZF13

Table of Contents

LAND OF THE SAMURAI

Long ago, the samurai warriors of Japan blazed onto battlefields. Local rulers called **daimyo** controlled Japan's many states. They hired these fierce fighters to help them protect their land.

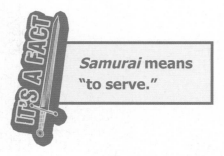

IT'S A FACT

Samurai means "to serve."

daimyo—a nobleman of Japan who owned a great deal of land

⬆ **Minamoto Yorimoto (on horse)**

In 1180 the Minamoto and Taira clans fought a war. The Minamoto won. Minamoto Yorimoto became Japan's first **shogun**. He controlled the emperor's samurai.

shogun—a military general who once
ruled Japan

Many daimyo wanted to
replace the shogun. Clans kept
fighting each other for power.
By the mid-1500s, samurai fought
constantly for their daimyo.
Respect for the samurai grew.

In ancient Japan, the shogun had more power than the emperor. The emperor was more of a religious leader.

GREAT WARRIORS

Fighting in battles brought rewards for the samurai. Daimyo gave them homes, land, and money. But not everyone could become a samurai. A man born outside the warrior **class** had to defeat a samurai to become one.

In 1591 the shogun made it illegal for people of other classes to become samurai.

class—a group of people in society with a similar way of life or income

↑ a samurai traveling with his servant

  a scene from the legend of the 47 ronin

Samurai worked different jobs for their daimyo. Fighting samurai fought on horseback or on foot. Housemen helped run the government instead of fighting. Samurai without masters were called ronin. They worked odd jobs.

IT'S A FACT

In the legend of the 47 ronin, a band of samurai get revenge for the killing of their master.

Samurai lived by a code called bushido.
Bushido means "the way of the warrior."
These rules controlled every part of a samurai's
life. According to the code, samurai had to be
willing to fight and die for their masters.

Many samurai studied poetry. They often wrote poems before fighting to prepare for death.

SAMURAI WEAPONS

Samurai went to battle in armor made of metal or leather. It covered nearly the entire body. Helmets looked like **demons** or animals about to attack.

A samurai's armor made him look much bigger than he really was.

demon—an evil spirit

Early samurai fought with bows and arrows. Bows were made of wood or bamboo. They measured 8 feet (2.4 meters) long. Later samurai began to rely more on their swords.

IT'S A FACT

Samurai often decorated and named their swords.

Samurai fought with other weapons too. They attacked enemies with spears called naginatas. A folding steel fan called a tessen was deadly in a samurai's hand. Samurai also mastered **martial arts**.

martial arts—styles of fighting or self-defense that come mostly from the Far East; tae kwon do, judo, and karate are examples of martial arts

a sword called a katana ➡

A samurai shouted his family name and rank during a battle. He looked for an enemy with an equal rank to fight.

　　Before a battle, the two sides faced
each other about 300 feet (90 m) apart.
The fight began with the wave of a baton
or flag. Samurai horsemen were the first
to charge into battle.

THE END OF THE SAMURAI

In 1543 Europeans brought the first guns to Japan. Samurai learned how to use them. But by 1725 the shogun had forced all **foreigners** out of Japan. He then outlawed guns and trade with other countries.

foreigner—a person who is staying or living in a country that is not his or her own country

IT'S A FACT

Japan's shoguns worried about citizens having guns. They feared that people would fight against the government.

In 1853 a U.S. naval officer convinced the shogun to open Japan's borders. The emperor disagreed with that decision. The samurai fought the shogun and returned power to the emperor.

U.S. naval officer Matthew Perry met with Japanese officials. He convinced the shogun to open Japan's borders.

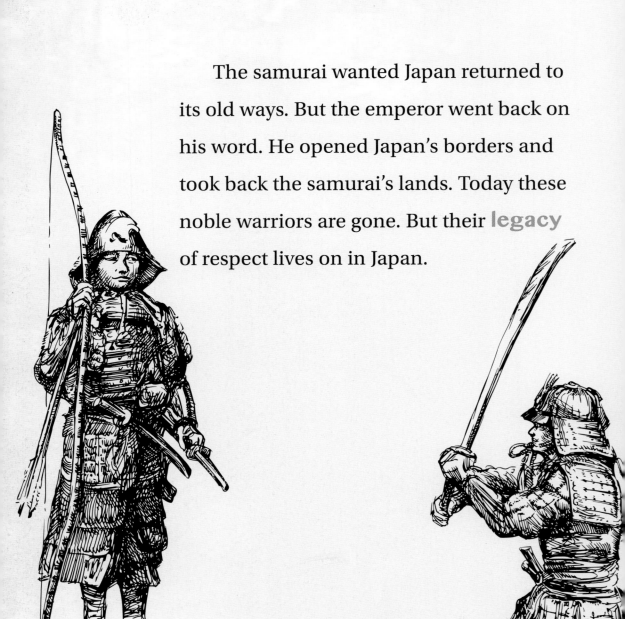

The samurai wanted Japan returned to its old ways. But the emperor went back on his word. He opened Japan's borders and took back the samurai's lands. Today these noble warriors are gone. But their legacy of respect lives on in Japan.

legacy—qualities and actions that one is remembered for; something that is passed on to future generations

A samurai named Takamori Saigo fought back against the emperor. Today statues honoring the brave samurai stand throughout Japan.

bushido (boo-SHE-doh)—a code of honor that demands loyalty and obedience and places honor before life

class (KLAS)—a group of people in society with a similar way of life or range of income

daimyo (DY-mee-oh)—a nobleman of Japan who owned a great deal of land

demon (DEE-muhn)—a devil or an evil spirit

foreigner (FOR-uhn-uhr)—a person who is staying or living in a country that is not his or her own country

legacy (LEG-uh-see)—qualities and actions that one is remembered for; something that is passed on to future generations

martial arts (MAR-shuhl ARTS)—styles of fighting or self-defense that come mostly from the Far East; tae kwon do, judo, and karate are examples of martial arts

shogun (SHOH-guhn)—a military general who once ruled Japan

Guillain, Charlotte. *Ninja.* Fierce Fighters. Chicago: Raintree, 2010.

Malam, John. *You Wouldn't Want to Be a Ninja Warrior!: A Secret Job That's Your Destiny.* New York: Franklin Watts, 2011.

McDaniel, Sean. *Ninja.* Torque: History's Greatest Warriors. Minneapolis: Bellwether Media, 2012.

INTERNET SITES

FactHound offers a safe, fun way to find Internet sites related to this book. All of the sites on FactHound have been researched by our staff.

Here's all you do:

Visit *www.facthound.com*

Type in this code: 9781476531137

Super-cool stuff! Check out projects, games and lots more at **www.capstonekids.com**